Book Disclaimer:

Please review the following agreement carefully before using this *"Enter The Steel Mace"* fitness program. The author strongly recommends that you consult with your physician before beginning any exercise program. You should be in good physical condition and be able to participate in the exercise.

Coach Vaughn is NOT a licensed medical care provider and represents no expertise in diagnosing, examining, or treating medical conditions of any kind, or in determining the effect of any specific exercise on a medical condition. You should understand that when participating in any exercise or exercise program, there is the possibility of physical injury. If you engage in this exercise or exercise program, you agree to do so at your own risk, are voluntarily participating in these activities, and assume all risk of injury to yourself, and agree to release and discharge Coach Vaughn from any and all claims or causes of action, known or unknown, arising out of negligence.

Self Published on Amazon's Kindle Direct Publishing of 2020

ABOUT COACH VAUGHN:

Coach Vaughn is from Palmdale, CA - based at Viking Valhalla Training Center providing professional one-on-one training for any goal. He has traveled all around the world learning from the best and practices his own craft before he teaches it. He's a certified fitness coach, Kettlebell Instructor, Flexible Steel, Stick Mobility Instructor and is a steel mace & club specialist. He writes articles, ebooks, and online certifications to help better educate fitness professionals as well with solid coaching cues broken down in detail. Anyone is welcome to Viking Valhalla Training Center if they are willing to learn.

 COACHVAUGHN.NET

 YouTube Subscribe : COACH VAUGHN

 coach_vikingvaughn

 viking valhalla training center

2

CHAPTER OUTLINE

CHAPTER 1

WHY THE STEEL MACE?

Have you ever noticed when walking into your typical corporate gym what is actually around you? Notice the majority of "strength machines" make you sit and have a screen installed on it or a mounted television above it. Anything that can make you go on auto-pilot. Then to add onto this, many blow up their ears with music and text on their smart phone during their "beast mode" workout. This consistent indulgence becomes a ritual habit to the point you can't focus without screens. To actually think and not be distracted is becoming a rare skill in this age. In the United States, the average American sits between 8-9 hours per day and spends the same amount of time (if not more) in front of a screen. Do we need MORE of this in an environment designed for real movement?

"ARE YOU MOVING POORLY BECAUSE YOU ARE IN PAIN, OR ARE YOU IN PAIN BECAUSE YOU ARE MOVING POORLY?"
– GRAY COOK

This is where the steel mace enhances that ability. Your mind & body must constantly stay connected to it. Whenever you're blasting music in your car and you all of a sudden get lost . . . you automatically turn down your music to now focus where you're going. Why? While hearing and seeing are two different senses, one can inhibit the other easily. Yet, many think "multitasking" is a productive method — when really they're just distracted going nowhere goal wise. This is a big reason steel maces are viewed as unconventional and even pointless to many because many gyms don't acknowledge the use of them.

However, well over a decade ago when I got into kettlebells they were also deemed the same, and now every gym has them because people see their true benefits. Steel maces are evolving the same way, but their educational path has not been truly defined yet. It's why many confuse them as the same thing as sledgehammers, and in doing so it's like comparing a landline phone against a smart phone. The features are completely different: head shape, handle length, and the material make a huge difference. An average sledgehammer also weighs no more than 15lb/7KG and a steel mace can go as heavy as 55lb/25KG. So a sledgehammer is not going to strengthen you staying at that low of a weight with a short handle length for steel mace training.

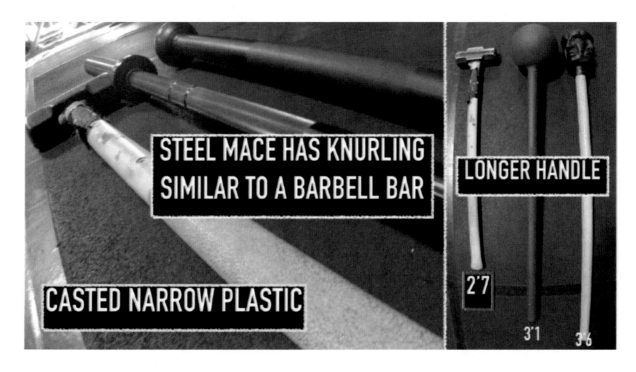

STEEL MACE HAS KNURLING SIMILAR TO A BARBELL BAR

LONGER HANDLE

CASTED NARROW PLASTIC

2'7

3'1   3'6

If you think a circular shape doesn't matter with steel mace training then why does it matter for other popular tools? Imagine clean & pressing a square barbell plate or snatching a rectangular like kettlebell? Your performance would be instantly affected all due to the shape. A mace builds a smooth centrifugal force with a complete 360 degree motion; contrast that to a square headed sledgehammer causing jagged 360 degree motions from the twisting and turning. The steel mace is also cast in one piece, making it safer to do tire strikes. I've unfortunately seen many tire strikes with a cheap sledgehammer and then the hammer head came flying off hitting someone else (a guaranteed lawsuit if you're training someone).

Steel Mace origins come from India and have been called Gadas for thousands of years in their culture. Gadas are as normal in India as kettlebells are in Russia. They cast a strong bamboo stick into a rounded molded concrete in a pot and use them for grappling strength for wrestling sport. Traditional Indian Gada methods are very shoulder dominant with primarily 360 motions with other asymmetrically loaded weight tools like Joris and Meels (giant wooden clubs). Gadas are typically much heavier with longer handles for these traditional strength training methods.

(XVII) Gada (Mace)

We hear and read many descriptions in Ramayan and Mahabharat about mace-fighting. Hanuman, Bhima, Duryodhan, Balaram, and others were the champions of mace-fighting in the age of Puranas. Mace fighting as such is not now in existence. Mace exercises however are current in Northern India. Mace includes a long handle and at one end, a heavy iron ball or stone ball is attached. Maces of varied heights and weights are devised for the use of persons of varied heights and strength.

From The Encyclopedia of Indian Physical Culture (1950)

Simply put, the Gada is a byproduct of globalization of many other cultures also seeing its true benefits until it meshed with western style barbell training, adding knurling grips and making it fully steel to make it more modern. With current trends of building garage gyms, and people working from home — steel maces have made a huge surge of popularity. While anyone could make a Gada, steel mace is much more affordable, compact, and easily shipped. In addition, steel mace offers much more variety of motion than giant Gada.

So to be clear, this book is for MODERN steel mace training methods to better correct posture and enlighten one's nervous system to use the right muscles at the right time with the steel mace's asymmetrical load in different movement positions. I respect the traditional Gada strength training methods, but at the same time I believe you can do far more with a steel mace than just perform constant shoulder dominant motions.

Saying modernizing the Gada into a steel mace is stupid — is like Black Sabbath calling Slayer stupid for advancing their Classic Heavy Metal doom sound with more speed and distortion, creating Thrash Metal. So like many of my favorite heavy metal bands, I'm taking a lot influences from mentors over the last decade traveling to their courses from around the world. If I had to describe the ingredients, I'm infusing Russian hardstyle strength training methods (as you would see with kettlebells) and physical therapy drills I've learned from the best doctors in the world to help prime your major joint systems and posterior chain muscles.

The steel mace was randomly introduced to me years ago attending Dr. Mark Cheng's course: *Prehab/Rehab*. What really gravitated me toward the steel mace was how little weight was needed to challenge my strength and I vividly remember not being able to do a simple 360 with 15lb because it was too heavy at the time. For an experienced lifter, that can military press a 48kg/106lb kettlebell, this was a bit of a shot for my ego to take. However, when I fail at something, it only makes me want to explore it more and I purchased 7lb, 10lb, and 15lb steel maces online as soon as I got back home from the course. At the time, there was absolutely zero educational content out there. If there was something it wasn't close to educational. I'll never forget clicking on a YouTube video with someone just holding a steel mace in a hoarded small room and saying "the steel mace helps stabilize your stabilizers to get more stability." The whole video was aimless biomechanical jargon and didn't demonstrate one exercise. So I immediately gave up looking online and started playing with the mace applying a lot of Pavel's Russian hard style strength methods.

As I experimented more with the steel mace in those months — it made me realize how much it related to sports that required ballistic actions like throwing, punching, and other striking patterns. It was also covering a lot of bases I was lacking that kettlebells couldn't cover. This is not to say steel maces are better than kettlebells.

Raw strength requires tension, but athletic feats require fluid mobility. While I love kettlebells — I had days where my body felt too tense from the training. The steel mace worked great for warm ups or easily doing a full workout while feeling it break up that post workout tension. The trick was how I was integrating it in 3-D movement patterns. What many don't realize is how linear typical exercises are and yet in sports we move side to side, rotate, resist rotation, reach, and strike with power. These patterns are very important for an athlete's injury prevention to not tear tendons or ligaments when moving in those dynamic planes of motion.

With the steel mace's asymmetrical load, it can help reduce bilateral imbalances we see now more than ever in many classic exercises. Barbell lifting is a great example of this because many push off one foot harder than the other with deadlifts or back squats due to an uneven lateral tilt happening in the hips (lacking tension from other posterior chain muscles). In my profession, the lats and obliques are the most under coached muscles and the glutes are the most over coached. Anyone can squeeze their butt checks together from an isolated training stand point, but can you tense them with your abs braced to protect your spine and lats packed to help maintain a torqued grip . . . ALL at the same time? Strength is a skill, so you need to view your workouts more as practice than as self punishment.

10

The goal of this book is to demonstrate dynamic and safe use of this unconventional tool. Each chapter is stacked in order to build you up at a safe pace and educate you on how it's not about just the tool, but the training philosophy behind it. This means that the same cues we use with the steel mace can easily be applied to your other favorite tools.

CHAPTER 2

SAFETY STANDARDS

So you're now looking online to buy steel maces and wondering "why are the weight selections so light?" This is what throws people off whether you're strong or just beginning. So you obliviously buy a 20lb mace, get it delivered a couple days later, and start playing around with it, and then realize "oh crap, this is TOO heavy for me." So why does this tool feel so heavy at first?

Wooden Custom made Steel Mace Rack

A steel mace is an asymmetrically (one side) loaded tool with all the weight in the mace head and no less than a pound in the handle. So we're not talking about a dumbbell or kettlebell here. Once you get the mace into the vertical stacked position your grip, lats (big muscle wings of the back anatomically known as the latissimus dorsi), and posture instantly gets challenged to resist the steel mace's gravitational pull being over your head. This is what makes the steel mace such a unique tool — you can increase your overall strength with little weight by exposing all the places you lack mobility or stability.

"So which steel mace is best for me then?" First, please be humble and take your ego out of the mix whether you're experienced with other tools or not. If you want to get the most out of your steel mace you need to pick a weight that allows you to do the most quality movements with it. The heavier you go, the less you can do with it. Another big thing many don't realize is steel mace training doesn't just train your muscles, but also your tendons and ligaments. Since they do not recover as fast as your muscles you need to be patient letting your tendons (especially in your elbows) get used to the weight you're using. The best weights for a beginner I've found are:

MEN	WOMEN
Under 200LB: *10LB Medium & 20LB Heavy*	Under 120LB: *7-10LB Medium & 15LB Heavy*
Over 200LB: *15LB Medium & 25LB Heavy*	Over 120LB: *10LB Medium & 20LB Heavy*

The medium mace will be best for learning all the movements in this book so you can focus on the technique and not the load. This is crucial to learning any tool so your nervous system can adapt to the feedback and not force it into positions you're not ready for. Then a heavy mace is best for the strength chapter of this book for offset pressing, bent over rows, dynamic lunges, and various squat positions. This will, in turn, make your medium mace feel lighter when you get into the 360 chapter.

So overall, the best pick is the 10lb mace for a beginner. Many companies also manufacture 7lb with a short handle. It's beneficial at first to have one, but overtime they become like training wheels and become worthless once experiencing yourself with heavier maces. Only if you're a fitness coach like myself should you have one to build up your students safely. Beginners will instantly notice jumping up 5lbs in weights makes a big difference with steel maces.

STEEL MACE SAFETY STANDARDS

1. FITNESS & HEALTH ARE NOT THE SAME

Do NOT perform any movements you feel uncomfortable with due to any health condition or injury. Please also consult with your doctor if you take medications for any condition that will contradict with this exercise program: high blood pressure, diabetes, heart conditions, or asthma, etc.

2. SAFE ENVIRONMENT / SAFE PERFORMANCE

Steel mace training in a residential home is NOT recommended because of ceiling height or possibly knocking into other fixtures. Either workout in a garage with optimal ceiling height or do it outside in your backyard or local park. Always be aware of your surroundings. Are you near an unlocked door someone can open? Are your kids or pets safely barricaded away from you when swinging a mace?

3. RACK STEEL MACES

While they easily can stand up balanced on the ground — all it takes is a is a tiny tap to knock them all over like bowling pins and crashing into other tools you don't want dents in. This is why I made a custom wooden wall mounted rack. However, horizontal barbell wall mount holders and Tornado hooks also work well to save space and keep your weight selections in order. If you do not want to use a rack — keep them grouped near a wall with no valuables near in case they tip over.

4. PERFORM BOTH SIDES

With the steel mace being an asymmetrically loaded tool you need to perform BOTH sides. For example, when vertically stacking the mace for 360's you'll perform it both directions by switching your grip and will require the same number of reps from both to equal one full set. So you would perform ten 360's to your right, switch your grip, perform another ten going to your left. Then safely set the mace down and rest in between sets. The same will be required for other positions like the front rack and athletically transitioning side to side in the prayer position.

PERFORM BOTH SIDES
TO EQUAL ONE SET

5. DO NOT EMBRACE THE "MORE, MORE, MORE" ATTITUDE

Doing hundreds of poor reps, too much weight, and 3+ hour workouts are all signs that point to inevitable injury. It's a complete myth in strength training that you need to "burn out" to attain major numbers. If you can throw a thousand punches, but none of them can knock me out . . . what's the point? While I can do hundred kettlebell snatches with a 28KG kettlebell in less than five minutes — did I do that every day to attain that skill? No! Focus more on solid reps of 10 and rest 1-2 minutes between sets. This keeps movement quality, power, and skills consistent. The same applies with any other fitness tool. If your following sets start to look ugly or feel off drop to a lower weight to keep your skill building consistent. So as an important rule, don't overload an exercise you wouldn't do with a medium steel mace.

15LB/ 7KG   55LB/25KG

IF YOU CAN'T DO IT WITH A MEDIUM MACE...
THEN YOU SHOULDN'T DO IT WITH A HEAVY MACE

CHAPTER 3

PRIME NINE
WARM UP

One of the dumbest things I did in my early 20's was overkill my warm ups with too much cardio. You know you're in Southern California when you see the gas prices and is the reason why I rode my bike nearly 20 miles round trip nearly everyday from home to a corporate gym. But was that enough for my former young & dumb self? Nope, after getting to the gym I would store the bike in the break room and then go on a 4 mile run around the local park outside. Only after doing all this, I would do my strength workout with kettlebells and bodyweight training back at the gym. Then I would do the same run again after and ride my bike home if I didn't have any training sessions.

During this time, I was into obstacle course runs and while my stamina held doing 8 to14 mile courses in crazy mountain terrain . . . I could not do ANY of the hanging obstacles: monkey bars, horizontal wall, and vertical rope climb. While this sounds stereotypical — my biggest weakness is I always work on strengths and not work on things I know I sucked at. I could do pushups all day, but hated pull ups (not being able to do one solid rep at the time) and used "I'm a big guy" excuse. After this realization, I simply worked on just tactical pull-ups consistently learning from others how to engage my lats. Guess what happened? I nailed all the climbing obstacles on the next the race without ever practicing on one. How? I owned the skill first, and this is why "more, more, more" attitude doesn't work for real strength. Treating a workout like practice ensures quality. Even when playing high school football, the team knew if we did poor on the practice field it was going to show on the game field Friday night. We all have the mental potential to do insanely hard workouts, but the real question is this workout maintainable to keep me consistent for the next one? So if your goal is to be sweaty and sore, go in a sauna and have someone beat you up. There's a reason why many professional sports teams do offseason training and lift heavier because now they're not at risk getting injured on the field. When professional athletes are in season for their sport — everything is skill based and they are not allowed to lift heavy during the season. So since we're focusing on steel mace training, we need to understand how the body needs to work with or without it.

To realign your posture and understand how your shoulders/hips internally and externally rotate isn't rocket science. In the following pages, we're going to breakdown how to get in a quick warm up priming all your major joint systems before we load them up in the strength chapter:

PRIME NINE SKILLS	REPS
Four Way Neck	5 REPS / All directions = 1 REP
Egyptians	10 REPS / Left to Right = 1 REP
Finger Waves	15-20 REPS / In & Out = 1 REP
Tea Cups	10 REPS Each Side
Half Kneeling Torso Rotations	10 REPS Each Side
Kettlebell Halos	10 REPS Left to right = 1 REP
Dead Bugs	10 REPS Left to right = 1 REP
Bird Dogs	10 REPS Left to right = 1 REP
Kettlebell Suitcase Carry	Walk 15-20 Yards Each Side

While there are a lot of other drills I'd love to show you — I need to keep it simple. Picking these *Prime Nine Drills* took a lot of thought because I want to address the body from head to toe. This warm up should not take more than 10 minutes. If you feel you need to do some form of cardio — do it after the workout. Save your strength to adapt to the steel mace first. If you cannot check off all nine drills with fluidity this will in turn affect your ability to control the steel mace (or else it controls you). For example, if you cannot halo a light kettlebell around your head without kipping your hips or ducking your neck . . . the same will happen with the 360 motion and will only worsen your technique. Connecting the dots with the skills required for steel mace training surprisingly doesn't require a steel mace.

Four Way Neck: Stand tall and clasp your hands together with your palms facing down. Try to extend your arms by pressing them toward the ground with your chest up. Once set, look left and right feeling your neck muscles stretch from the top notch of your chest. Then up and down feeling your shoulders prying in place keeping your hands in place. This addresses many issues we see with desk jobs and being on one's phone in a forward flexed position.

UP

DOWN

CLASP HANDS
BEHIND

LEFT

RIGHT

Egyptians: Start raising your arms to shoulder level with both palms down. Keep your knees soft (flexed) and pivot one foot at a time looking toward the palm up hand. The other rotates palm up as well, but from the shoulder internally rotating. Be sure to dig the toes down like "squishing a bug." Then come back to the start and go to the other side. You'll notice one side will not rotate as good as the other, but now being aware of it you can work on this bilateral imbalance.

Finger Waves: Hold your hands out in front with the fingers grasped in (elbows can be flexed) palm down. Then rotate and extend each finger outward — then smoothly flex each finger inward palm up. Repeat back to the other direction keeping your shoulders and elbows stable. You will notice when performing steel mace 360s you will need to grasp the handle with only the index & thumb in the pendulum phase. This drill helps prevent death gripping the steel mace — so you can do this in between sets as many times as you'd like.

22

Tea Cups: Hold your hand out to your side palm up. Using a ball is optional, but helps keep your palm up as you rotate in toward your torso and back outward creating space hinging your hips back. However, many cheat cupping or grasping the ball by picture 4. Keep your fingers spread out just like holding a tea cup on a plate as you rotate your palm in and out - coming back to the original start position each time to repeat it. This drill is a must for those with elbow and shoulder issues. Once again, you'll notice one side will not be as mobile as the other and it is your job to work on it consistently.

<u>Half Kneeling Torso Rotations:</u> Start in a half kneeling position with your rear foot toes dug down to keep the hips extended (do not fold the hips into your low back). The front leg's shin remains vertical. Have your hands connected together in a prayer position at the sternum. Then as you rotate the torso extend your arms out as far as you can. Collapse your hands and torso back in to the start position and rotate to the other side. The goal is to rotate with thoracic extension (mid back) and not compensate using your hips. You'll notice your legs will want to shift open so your low back can move with more rotation than your thoracic spine. Perform both sides in half kneeling position and move with control — not speed.

Kettlebell Halos: Grab a light kettlebell by the horns (upside down). Push the kettlebell around your head until it's fully behind your back side — feeling the long head of the triceps lengthen with the lats as it rotates. Pull the kettlebell in keeping the shoulders away from the ears until it comes back to the start position. Then push it back in the other direction equalling one rep. Do not rush this drill or use a heavy kettlebell. If you do not have a kettlebell — clasp your hands together in the same start position and halo your hands around your head instead. This is a prerequisite before ever attempting the steel mace 360. Keep the ribs hidden down not flaring and the hips stable with no back and forth shifting to compensate the lack of range of motion from the shoulders.

PUSH AROUND HEAD NOT DUCKING | FEEL TRICEPS & LATS LENGTHEN | PULL KEEPING SHOULDERS AWAY FROM EARS | PUSH BACK IN OTHER DIRECTION

It is a huge myth in steel mace training that 360s help reduce shoulder pain. Yes, they help keep them resilient, but chronic pain is a completely different story. The shoulder capsules have tissues called labrums (as well as the hip capsules) to help articulate in different positions and keep the sockets from being dislocated. However, if your arms and shoulders are getting pulled and bashed into these positions without using your lats and other prime posterior chain muscles this causes tearing of the shoulder labrum overtime. The steel mace's weight can double or even triple in the pendulum phase from the accelerated force and if the lats aren't mobile and strong enough to take that — the shoulder labrum takes the force every time until pain tells you to stop.

Dead Bugs: Lie down in a supinated quadruped position with your knees stacked over your hips and hands over your shoulders. Once braced, "hiding your ribs down" — extend one arm and leg from the opposite side. So the right arm raises back and left leg extends. You'll come back to the start position and repeat to the other side. This exercise teaches to engage the back extensor muscles of the posterior chain to give greater core stiffness. As you see in the images on the right, the red lines indicate the force I want Amanda to resist and the green lines where I want her to stabilize using her lats and glutes to attain bracing. This is called "reciprocal inhibition," and is a great way for fitness coaches to teach what muscles you want to enforce proper joint alignment in a safe controlled manner.

The biggest stereotypical myth in fitness is you need to do hundreds of floor crunches to attain a strong core. Many worship the "6 pack" to a lean stomach and false media attains this myth to keep you buying products to "burn fat with no effort." Fat targeting an area on your body is like saying you're going to target a freckle on the body as well. Any pro physique bodybuilder will tell you it all comes down to your nutritional habits, good sleep, and making your own food in the kitchen to attain a leaner look. However, this is not a nutrition book and I'm no spokesperson on show off abs. I'm more trying to educate you that anatomically speaking the human core musculature accounts for 29 different muscles that wrap around your entire body and go from your mid chest to mid quad. Not only that, but your core works diagonally. Performing floor crunches do nothing but complete the task of bringing your rib cage toward your pelvis with a passive forward flexed spine (and painfully pulling your neck into forced flexion). Wait, forward flexed spine? Like the daily dosage we already get enough of being on our phones and desktops all day? My point is core strength is deemed on bettering your performance — not blinding it with soreness.

The Dead Bug & Bird Dog are from Dr. Stuart McGill's book, Ultimate Back Fitness & Performance. Highly recommend if you're interested learning how the spine works under scientific evidenced based exercise

Bird Dogs: All we're doing now is flipping the quadruped position with the hands and toes rooted to the ground. However, the dead bug uses the ground for feedback if it's tilted to maintain alignment. Using a ball statically placed on the lumbar is a perfect feedback tool to maintain stability and alignment. The key to doing so is before lifting your opposite limbs into extension is rooting your hands into the floor like "opening two pickle jars." This externally rotates your arms (showing your elbow pits) into your lats and pushes your neck into extension with an open neck. Then dig your toes down feeling all four limbs connecting to the floor. Once set with this in mind, kick back one heel and have the opposite arm reaching as far as you can without compromising losing the ball on your low back. Do not cheat this by rib flaring to help cusp the ball better — "hide your ribs down" just as we did in the dead bug.

Notice in both the dead bug and bird dog we just corrected the issues we commonly see in the squat. "But don't we need to squat in order to correct it?" No, if you flip Amanda's quadruped position upright . . . what position do you see? While we'll get more into proper squats with the steel mace in various positions in the next chapter — I cannot tell you how many trainers are overkilling their clients with pointless boxes behind them, heel raised platforms, and the holy "booty band" wrapped around the knees. If you need 3-4 different tools to correct ONE movement pattern you don't understand how the human body works.

> ## "THE BODY WORKS AS ONE PIECE. IT'S NOT BUILT LIKE FRANKENSTEIN."
> ## – Dan John

DO NOT TILT LOW BACK

DIG & ROOT TOES

"OPEN TWO PICKLE JARS"

KICK HEEL BACK ENGAGING GLUTE

REACH WITH ARM CONNECTED TO LAT

REPEAT ON OTHER SIDE

<u>Kettlebell Suitcase Carry</u>: Deadlift a kettlebell by hinging your hips back first with a flat back. Securely grip the kettlebell with your thumb and fingers fully wrapped around the handle — do NOT loosely grip with the palm showing. Then drive the kettlebell up by fully extending your hips and locking your loaded arm into your lat (notice how Amanda's elbow pit is externally rotated and isn't pointing toward her torso). Once vertically planked, you should feel the kettlebell's load trying to pull you toward it by tilting your torso. Resist as if someone was going to punch your opposite oblique (top picture). You will then walk tall pressing your toes into the floor. Do not walk with flat feet, stiff knees, or slouch toward the kettlebell. Breathe normally and maintain abdominal bracing — this is called "breathing behind the shield." If you do not have a kettlebell use a dumbbell or anything heavy to give you enough of a challenge.

Using a light weight will not do much with carries. Ladies, do not be afraid of lifting heavier weights. That is another myth that really peeves me around arrogant male meat head egos. I find it repulsive and offensive to women in general when male trainers hand a female client 5lb weights. I've had women carry 32kg kettlebells easily as men stare insecurely during their beloved bicep workouts:

- Men should be able to lift a 32kg/70lb weight or higher
- Women should be able lift a 20kg/40lb weight or higher

As we've learned so far, the core works in 3-D and not in one crunched linear plane. A big part of this program is having not only the grip strength to control the steel mace, but resisting the forces it creates around your body. This simple drill has great carryover to keep your grip strength and posture in check.

BRACE OPPOSITE OBLIQUE AS IF YOU WERE TAKING A PUNCH

WALK TALL ✓

LAZY ✗

31

CHAPTER 4

STEEL MACE
STRENGTH

While the steel mace serves as a great ballistic tool (swings) - they also perform incredibly well for rows, squats, presses, and other dynamic movements. Learning and practicing to create more tension for these classic lifts can lead to stronger gains. However, death gripping is an involuntary emergency brake from the nervous system and we want to learn how to properly crush, torque, and pull the mace to enforce proper engagement. So how do we make this voluntary? In this chapter, we're going to break down the best ways and change the way you view these common strength exercises making them even better utilizing the steel mace's offset weight.

Since a good portion of the steel exercises we'll be covering will involve a solid hip hinge pattern we need to cover how to properly do it without compromising your spine first. Biomechanically, a hip hinge is minimal knee flexion with maximal hip flexion. A squat requires both maximal flexion from the knee and hip. So the hips push back in the hinge and the hips go down in the squat. This is why many swing kettlebells poorly with no power squatting into the movement or look like a dog taking a dump when barbell deadlifting all because the hips are too low with a flexed spine. Instead we're going to build the hip hinge pattern first so we can have a solid foundation to start and rid any strength leaks before progressing them into other strength exercises.

> **"MOVEMENT IS JUST LIKE MONEY.**
> **YOU CAN MAX YOUR CREDIT CARD,**
> **BUT SOONER OR LATER YOU WILL PAY THE BILL".**
> **– DR. MARK CHENG**

Stick Hip Hinge: Place a single stick against your spine and feel the stick make contact with the top of your head, mid, and low back. One hand will grip the top palm down and the other will grip below palm up. Once set in a stable vertical plank, slowly push your hips back and maintain all of the three points of contact. You'll notice one of the three will want to create more space to cheat the hip hinge for more range. Remember, it's a hip hinge — not a squat.

MAINTAIN ALL THREE POINTS OF CONTACT AS YOU HIP HINGE

RIB FLARING   NECK FLEXION   LUMBAR FLEXION

<u>Offset Deadlifts:</u> Fully grip the steel mace's handle with both palms down thinking of the same vertical plank you started with in the stick hip hinge. Now "break the bar" to externally rotate your arms into your lats and this action should automatically retract your shoulders down with a longer neck.

Creating this torque should also show visible flexion from the tricep area and connects you with the mace as one moving piece. Now push your hips back keeping the handle near your shins to maintain a neutral spine. You should feel the hamstrings lengthening and lats keeping the shoulders over the handle. Slight extension is okay at the bottom, and keep your eyes looking six feet ahead. Once at your optimal range, drive the hips into extension coming back locked into the vertical plank with your lats, glutes, and abdomen braced.

Offset Bent Over Rows: Set up a static hip hinge position with your mace hand (the one closest to the mace head) palm down and the arm extended. The base hand (furthest from the mace head) is also palm down, but the elbow is flexed to offset the steel mace diagonally — making it an anti-rotation exercise. Keep your shoulders and hips square as you row the *mace hand* up and push down with the *base hand*.

MACE HAND PULLS   BASE HAND PUSHES

LOOK 6FT
AHEAD
MAINTAINING
STATIC HIP
HINGE

ROW IN TIGHT
NEAR RIBS
&
RESIST
TWISTING
TORSO WITH
KNEES
MINIMALLY
FLEXED

<u>Dynamic Curls</u>: Start with the hands lengthened and actively pressing into the handle — just below the mace head. While in the Prayer Position, it should be aligning to your spine and will be the transitional point to switch each hand from palm up to down. The mace hand (closest to the mace head) should be palm up with the arm extended and externally rotated into the lat. The base hand (furthest from the mace head) should be palm down with the arm bent at the elbow. The body should remain tall and NOT tilt toward the mace head letting it control you as it transitions left to right. Tossing the mace up and over head as it slams back into your hands is not recommended. Practicing this is essential to build them into lunge and squat patterns with fluidity.

← MACE HAND PALM UP   PRAYER POSITION   BASE HAND PALM DOWN →

Sumo Side Lunges: Start in a wide stance, and have the mace vertically aligned with your spine in the prayer position. Slide the base hand palm down as the mace hand slides palm up near the mace head simultaneously going into a side lunge for both sides. The extending leg should align with the steel mace as the other bends to help push the hips back into a more lateral hip hinge position. Keep both feet rooted to the floor by actively pressing them into the floor as you smoothly transition left to right.

TRANSITION WITH PRAYER POSITION IN WIDE STANCE

CONTOUR TO EXTENDING LEG

38

Offset Military Press: Set up in a strong front rack position fully gripping the handle with the wrists neutral and forearms vertical. Lock your knees and hips by engaging your quads and glutes to keep a level belt line as you press the steel mace over head. Fully lock out your arms maintaining a neutral wrist. Just like the kettlebell suitcase carry you will need to resist tilting by firing your opposite oblique.

KEEP WRISTS NEUTRAL
WITH VERTICAL FOREARMS

FRONT RACK

FULLY
LOCKOUT
ARMS
&
RESIST
TILTING

Partner Lat Pack Drill: Stereotypically, many think of overhead pressing as an isolated shoulder muscle recruitment stand point and more so don't know how to use bigger muscles like the lats, abs and glutes at the same time to create more strength output (or muscle recruitment). Once partner A fully offset military presses overhead — Partner B will press into Part A's elbows to enforce a pull effect into the lats (like a strict pull up) to better reset into the lats for each rep. As Partner A is pulling down, the glutes need to be squeezed to keep the hips level and then "hide the ribs down" so the ribs to do not flare.

Lap & Front Squats: Now understanding how to control the steel mace in multiple positions we can take those same cues into squats. What I love about the steel mace is it can easily transition into a squat variation you see from a barbell to kettlebell standpoint. When squatting down think of "pulling your torso in between your hips" and pushing your knees out to create more space for your torso. Then, engage your lats to maintain thoracic extension needed at the bottom of the squat. Many fold in like an accordion and go down with no range (which is why we did the stick hip hinge first).

LAP SQUAT
TRANSITION WITH PRAYER POSTION

FRONT SQUAT
TRANSITION WITH VERTICAL STACK

"BREAK THE BAR"
NEAR THE STERNUM

MAINTAIN FRONT RACK LIKE
THE TOP OF A PULL UP

Press Out Squats: Start in the vertical position getting your shoulders down and back. As you squat down (just below knee to hip), actively press out the mace slowly extending your arms until your elbow pits are pointing up (externally rotated). To do this correctly you need to "break the bar" using the lats to keep it locked out and to keep it stacked over your hands. The mace head should not tilt toward your head or flex your wrists back (which therefore makes your elbows bend and lose the lat connection). Once you come back up extending your hips actively pull the mace back in to the vertical stack position. As the glutes squeeze, you also need to think about connecting them with your lats and abdomen braced for the entire set.

The goal as you come down from the squat is to simply keep the mace stacked over your hands the whole time. Once again, don't confuse simple with easy. Now keeping the mace vertical, this forces you to squat down correctly with full range of motion from the knees and hips. The mace's vertical position also represents your spine to stay strong, tall, and upright. If you have an issue maintaining this you can either choke up on the mace or use a shorter handled mace (Jemena is using a short 7lb mace on the right).

This is also a great corrective for poor 360s for the same reason many do poor squats — they go too fast with lazy repetitions. For this reason, I will never be a fan of social media influenced "squat challenges" in which you perform hundreds of poor repetitions each day to complete a desired number in a month. With trends like this it's no surprise people are now doing the same with "steel mace 360 challenges" and stereotyping it with this one exercise. Everyone I've coached who have done these types of challenges always have a bursitis hip issue or tendonosis issue from over use not taking any rest days. I can goblet squat a 80kg/176lb kettlebell for reps, but can I do that everyday for a month? No, I simply schedule one day out of the week to squat low reps and focus on solid technique.

FULLY LOCKOUT ARMS KEEPING MACE STACKED OVER HANDS BY "BREAKING THE BAR" AS YOU SQUAT

Goblet Squats: Set up the mace vertically, but now have one hand on top of the mace head and the other still on the base handle. Once set, reverse the mace head down toward the ground as you squat. At the bottom, pull your base hand in and push your mace hand tossing it into the vertical stack position and repeat on the next side. Notice how the mace is still vertical at the top and bottom position of the squat, but only reversed up and down. You will then switch hands performing the other side.

This is where your transition skills with the steel mace will be tested. What I love about this variation is the push and pull effect we've been doing with the dynamic curl now gets literally flipped upside down.

VERTICAL STACK

REACH ONE HAND UP

FLIP DOWN ALIGNING TO SPINE

SQUAT KNEE TO HIP

FLIP BACK UP TO VERTICAL STACK

REPEAT ON OTHER SIDE

CHAPTER 5

MASTERING THE 360
WITH THE FOUR P's

Now that we've culminated a solid foundation of not just how to control the steel mace in multiple positions, but how to use all the muscles you didn't know how to use during workouts. This is why I do NOT recommend beginners go straight into doing steel mace 360s. While I love 360s, they're becoming extremely stereotyped as the only exercise to do with steel maces and can do more damage than good when performing them like a robot with zero emphasis on technique. If you're jerking your neck and hips forward as the mace rotates around you this is a big sign you're not ready to do them because it's controlling you to the point of inevitable injury.

The shoulder girdle can work in many dynamic articulations, but the thoracic spine (mid back) also plays a big part in unlocking those ranges to complete a fluid steel mace 360. So if you're in a forward flexed position all day on a smart phone or desk job don't blame the steel mace. This is why the *Prime Nine* are set as movement standards to be maintained. If a friend wanted to drive your manual car, but they only knew how to drive automatic . . . would you let them drive it? No, because that person would likely jack up your transmission all because they didn't want to learn the skills on how to do it. That's how I feel when I see someone doing poorly swung 360s right off the bat. View your shoulders like a car's transmission — you can't force the gears into speeds it's not ready for and will only transition to the next gear at the right time and speed.

So after years of coaching this specific exercise I developed the Four P's to hit all the check points needed to do each 360 with solid technique: Push, Pendulum, Pull, and Pause.

PUSH: Set up in the vertical stack position and point with the base hand signaling the direction you're going in. From here you want to push the mace AROUND your shoulders to set up the pendulum phase. Pushing it over the shoulders enforces you to shrug and lose space in your neck.

POINT YOUR BASE INDEX FINGER TO SIGNAL THE DIRECTION IT'S GOING

PUSH AROUND SHOULDERS

NOT OVER SHOULDERS

PENDULUM: Practicing this alone can help build the thoracic extension and fluid like grip needed to make your 360s smoother and not jagged looking. Since you can't see the mace once it's behind you many fear of it hitting their butt and death grip thinking this will prevent it. First, if it hits your butt (it really doesn't hurt) this means your hyperextending your low back. So view it as tactical feedback from the steel mace saying "STOP using your low back to swing me!"

LET THE MACE NATURALLY BUILD THE ARC BY GRIPPING WITH INDEX & THUMB

The pendulum needs uninterrupted acceleration to build a smooth arc and the trick is to grip with your index & thumb. Just like with kettlebell cleans — your hands need to relax for a split second so the bell can rotate around the wrist or else it slams against your forearm from death gripping.

PULL: This is where the lats need to take over the accelerated force from the pendulum. With that said, I've never been a fan of shouldering the mace handle because it puts more emphasis on loading your spine with excessively rounded torso rotation. For classic Gada training, this shouldering technique works better because smooth handled wood/bamboo is more forgiving than the knurled steel gliding across your clavicle's skin. To enforce this needed lat contraction and to challenge your vertical plank I came up with the Banded 10 & 2:

PAUSE: The biggest mistake beginners make with 360s is going too fast and this, in turn, causes shoulder impingement and elbow pain for doing too many reps this fast. This also takes away the centrifugal force needed to maintain the 360 degree motion smoothly and sends it into more jagged directions (bottom). All you have to do is PAUSE in the vertical stack position for a slight second before you repeat the process. This gets your grip stronger and resets your shoulders to make sure they're not elevating up toward the neck. As Bruce Lee famously states: "if you can't do it slow . . . then you can't do it fast."

PUSHING OVER YOUR
SHOULDERS MAKES YOU
USE YOUR TRAPS

THEREFORE CAUSING
DEATH GRIPPING IN
THE PENDULUM PHASE

EXCESSIVE TORSO ROTATION
ROUNDING SPINE
WITH NO CONTROL

= NOT MAINTAINABLE & SHOULDERS WILL HATE YOU

Putting It All Together — **<u>Two Hand (2H) 360</u>:**

PUSH AROUND SHOULDERS

**PENDULUM
USING INDEX & THUMB**

Mastering The Four P's For Steel Mace 360s:

Please watch this video tutorial by scanning this QR code on your mobile device.

**PULL WITH LATS
RESISTING ROTATION**

**PAUSE & RESET
VERTICAL STACK**

<u>Half Kneeling 360s:</u> This a great corrective for those shifting the hips during the pendulum phase. Start in a half kneeling position, vertically stack the steel mace and push your base hand away from the front leg and toward the rear leg (this gives you more space). By digging down your rear big toe into the ground this fully extends the hips and locks them in with the glutes tight. You should feel an active stretch from the hip flexor going down your thigh on the grounded knee.

PUSH MACE AWAY FROM FRONT LEG   **PUSH AROUND SHOULDERS**   **PENDULUM WHILE REAR LEG IS DUG DOWN WITH TOES**

Once done, switch legs and switch your vertical stack position to push in the other direction.

54

As a key note here, this half kneeling position is not just exclusive to 360s. You can also do kettlebell halos and offset military presses to prevent excessive leaning.

**PULL WITH LATS KEEPING
SPINE & HIPS UPRIGHT**

**PAUSE IN
VERTICAL STACK**

90/90 Hip Press 360s: Sit down with a tall spine and have your front leg externally rotated and the rear leg internally rotated (both at a 90 degree angle). This position is challenging by itself because now your spine wants to lean away from the internally rotated rear leg to make more space in your lumbar — which is what we don't want. Grab the mace, setting up in the vertical stack position (bottom right on the next page is your start & finish) once you feel your hip capsules/spine are in alignment. Then drive your knees into the floor and fully extend your hips with tight glutes to maintain it when you push and pendulum the mace (top left & right). This makes your glutes work harder to work with your lats to maintain a neutral spine resisting the mace's rotational force. Once you pull the mace in own your pause in the vertical stack and then gently sit down by hinging your hips to the ground (with both legs still in the 90/90 position). After switching your legs and your grip do the next side.

This is a great corrective for those that go too fast and shift their hips with a forward knee scoop during a 360. Performing it like so clearly demonstrates unnecessary load on the lumbar spine. This is one of the many reasons why the steel mace 360s should NOT be viewed as an "upper body" or "shoulder workout." Any poor movement pattern that affects the hips will also go upstream kinetically.

PUSH AWAY FROM REAR LEG   PENDULUM KEEPING HIPS EXTENDED

PULL   PAUSE IN VERTICAL STACK & SIT DOWN

Kneeling 360 Complex: Start in the tall kneeling position (both knees down) and grab the steel mace in the vertical stack position. Perform a 360 and then lift one leg up into the half kneeling position performing another 360 pushing your base hand away from the front leg. Then dig and push off rear your foot to stand up tall with a level belt line performing another 360. Then reverse back down performing 360s in the half and tall kneeling position again. Switch your grip in the vertical stack and lift the other leg up in the half kneeling to perform both sides (both sides equals one set).

To be clear, you're performing 360s ONE AT TIME in each position as you go up and down (starting and ending in the tall kneeling position). One set should equal ten 360 reps (so each side is five reps). I consider this kneeling 360 complex to be a prerequisite before advancing into single arm variations because it demonstrates fluidity to step up and down with control.

REVERSE BACK DOWN

ONCE BACK IN TALL KNEELING, SWITCH GRIP AND USE OTHER LEG IN HALF KNEELING TO PERFORM BOTH SIDES

STANDING

HALF KNEELING
(PUSH AWAY FROM FRONT LEG)

TALL KNEELING

10&2's: A 360 goes in one direction, and I've gotten a lot of comments saying "but this person says you should push with the top hand and not your base hand." The fact is, it doesn't matter because if you plan on advancing your 360 skills then 10 & 2's will naturally evolve by traveling in both directions. This variation requires more speed by taking out the vertical stack position with no pause until you're done. As stated in the safety standards chapter, when performing the vertical stack position —you do BOTH sides by switching your hands.

ENVISON A CLOCK AROUND YOU AND HIT THE 10 & 2 O'CLOCK SPOTS EACH REP

Over the past years, I've sadly seen "mace competitions" accept this type of technique as a completed repetition to get as many 10 & 2's as possible in a five minute time span. In kettlebell sport competitions, the judge will only count jerks and snatches when the elbow FULLY locks out overhead. If the kettlebell judge says "no count" multiple times they can also disqualify the athlete for poor technique. However, this has become ignored with competition mace 10 & 2's and an athlete can cheat a 10 & 2 by not fully pulling the bottom of the handle near the torso — making it a 9 & 3. It looks weak as the hips and knees constantly shift back & forth (this also causes serious elbow tendon issues). In contrast, it's like someone half repping a bench press (slightly bending and extending their elbows) and never touching the bar to the chest at full range.

HIPS SHOULD NOT KIP FORWARD AS YOU SWING MACE

IT'S NOT A 9 & 3!
FINISH AT FULL RANGE

One Hand (1H) 360s: Once you become confident with the two handed variations doing 1H 360s are very handy to make your medium sized steel mace feel heavy all over again. However, the same standards remain as we did with the 2H 360s. The main difference is using your free hand to spot the steel mace before and after each rep to get used to pausing it safely. Once you get the groove of it you don't have to use your free hand.

SAME STANDARDS
DIFFERENT CONDITIONS

PUSH   PENDULUM   PULL   PAUSE

Hand to Hand (H2H) 10 & 2's: Start just as you would be performing a 1H 360, but now pull harder toward the belly button decelerating the mace for a split second in the 10 & 2 position so the other hand can grip it and swing in the other direction. Try not let the free hand sway too far away from the mid line of your body and keep it near your belly button so the H2H switch is smooth during each rep. When performing, think you do not want the mace to go near your face in the 12 o'clock position. The triceps and lats really get worked with this H2H variation. So it's recommended you swing no longer than 30-45 seconds when first practicing.

If you feel shoulder or elbow pain with this, it's heavily recommend you try subbing them with Indian Club Mill Drills (featured in Chapter 8). I added Indian Clubs into this book because a huge myth has brewed over the past few years that steel maces can "help rid shoulder issues with 360s" — which I highly disagree with. Once again, there's a reason why the *Prime Nine* is set as a movement standard for this book so you don't hurt yourself or worsen a chronic injury. The steel mace can help keep your shoulders resilient in many articulations, but this is a completely different story when chronic pain is involved. The steel mace's long handle requires good thoracic mobility in the pendulum position and usually everyone that has shoulder issues also has thoracic spine issues (usually being rounded from a sedentary lifestyle). So the Indian club's short handle is a perfect substitute to better control thoracic extension needed to let the shoulder capsule move freely in these articulations similar to the steel mace.

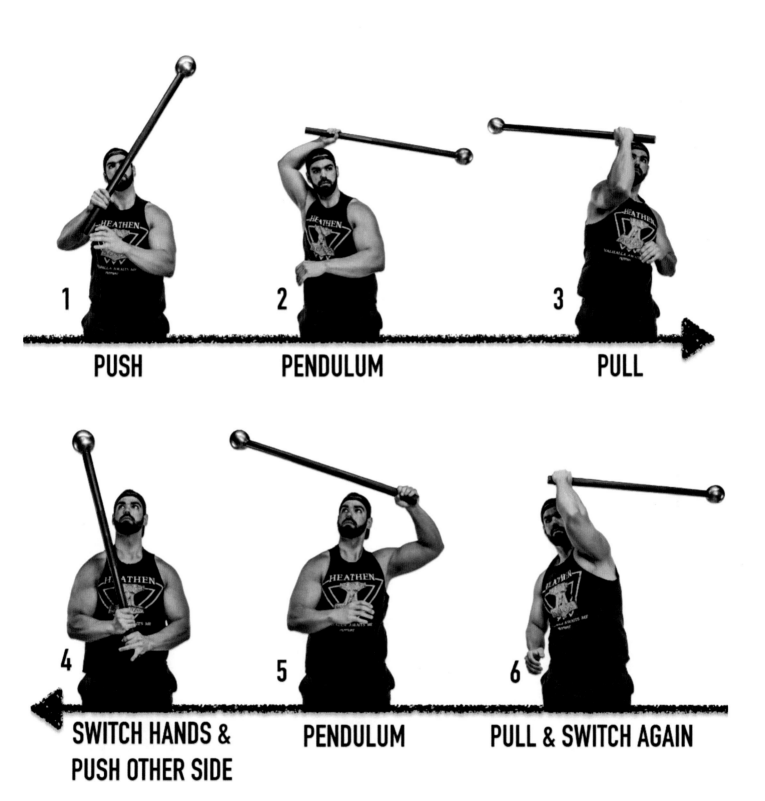

1 PUSH

2 PENDULUM

3 PULL

4 SWITCH HANDS & PUSH OTHER SIDE

5 PENDULUM

6 PULL & SWITCH AGAIN

CHAPTER 6

SWING & CATCHES

Whenever a new tool becomes popular it's no surprise people start treating it like a hammer and see everything as a nail. A perfect example is people online swinging steel maces in between their legs like a kettlebell. It's the same thing as someone banging in a screw with a hammer . . . everyone knows a screwdriver is more effective. Just because you can doesn't mean you should. However, with the steel mace's longer handle and spherical head it can still be put to use with swings beyond just 360 motions. Swing & Catches are a great change up in taming the arc now around your body in a different plane. This is also another reason why steel maces should not be confused as the same thing as a sledge hammer because, once again, the head shape and handle length will not work for this exercise.

What I love about steel mace Swing & Catches is the ability to train finger and hand dexterity. When in the back swing phase, the steel mace is off to the side and your hand must now conform to its shape (like holding a torch). Then after an explosive hip hinge (similar to a hard style kettlebell swing) making it weightless for a slight second, the hand must gently relax to travel up to the mace head and grip its spherical shape with all fingers. Not everything we grip in everyday life is perfectly symmetrically balanced with a sturdy handle. This is something most strength coaches don't talk about enough as we age, yet issues like arthritis/osteoporosis are only growing because we don't do simple exercises like Swing & Catches. There is a reason why I implemented Kettlebell Suitcase carries and Finger Waves in the *Prime Nine* drills to prep you for this exercise.

Never confuse simple with easy because now more than ever people judge a book by it's cover (with no real experience themselves). So while this exercise looks easy — performing it with consistent power, rhythm, and fluidity is not. As we did in the last chapter we will work on the foundational basics one side at a time before going into the hand to hand variation.

1H Deadstop Swing: Before you catch the mace you need to learn how to swing it first by using your hips ballistically. Set up by hinging your hips back putting most of the weight into your heels and actively gripping the floor with your toes. The mace should be on one side outside the hips and grasp it like a torch (with the wrist extended along the handle). The further your hand is away from the mace head the heavier it will feel, so find a perfect spot you can manage as you swing. Once set, hike the mace into the back swing and explode up by fully extending your hips, squeezing the glutes tight while the lat (on the mace side) is retracting the shoulder down and back. The mace should feel weightless as your body is vertically planked (middle photo). As soon as the arm connects back to your side, quickly hinge your hips back to decelerate the mace in the back onto the ground. If it slams onto the ground this shows you're pulling the mace with your arm and less with ballistic hip power (pulling & swinging are not the same). If you can't make your start look like your finish with this 1H deadstop swing you don't have the green light to advance to the swing & catch variations.

| HIP HINGE TILTING MACE | BACK SWING | EXPLODE UP EXTENDING HIPS | BACK SWING | DEADSTOP MACE BACK TO START |

As an important safety note before we advance on the next pages, always Swing & Catch the steel mace off to your sides . . . NOT near your face. This throws off the arc and will not end well if it does hit your face. If you avoid this advice then up your dental insurance.

UNLESS YOU WANT TO SEE A DENTIST....
DO NOT SWING MACE HEAD NEAR FACE!

1H Swing & Catch: Set up the steel mace on one side and have it tilted on the ground so you can load up into your hip hinge position (as we did with the stick). Most of the weight should be on your heel when starting, but once you feel your hips are hinged with a neutral spine splay and grip the ground with your toes to keep them rooted to the ground (the feet should NOT rock back & forth as you swing). Notice on the first photo my elbow pit is externally rotated out and my lat on that side is packed to keep my shoulder connected with my torso. Once set, hike the mace back looking six feet ahead with slight neck extension and explode up extending your hips ballistically (as you would jumping up). This "pop & float" action makes the steel mace weightless so your hand can fluidly slide up to the mace head.

SET UP HIP HINGE
WITH MACE AT
SIDE TILTED

HIKE BACK LOOKING 6FT
AHEAD WITH SLIGHT
NECK EXTENSTION

"POP & FLOAT" UP
BY SLIDING HAND
UP TO MACEHEAD

With your palm and fingers widened in this split second — fully grasp the mace head by actively crush gripping it to stabilize it at the top of the swing with a solid catch. Your wrist can flex back a bit, but do not let the bottom handle arc up any higher above your head. Once in the vertical plank, flick your wrist forward letting go of the steel mace for another split millisecond to transition back to the handle grasping it firmly as you hinge your hips back again to repeat the process. As you get better with the "pop & float" you'll notice you can add more air to it with less emphasis sliding your hand up.

CATCH BY FULLY GRIPPING WITH ALL FINGERS

FLICK WRIST & SLIDE HAND BACK TO HANDLE

REPEAT

Hand to Hand (H2H) Swing & Catch: Once you feel you've got the groove down and smoothly transitioning your hands from the handle to the mace head you can evolve it side to side. The big difference is the arc now needs to travel in a horse shoe like shape with the "pop & float" phase to transition to the other hand. Also, notice below how my shoulders & hips are stacked over each other in the hip hinge from right to left. Your torso should not rotate toward the steel mace to compensate for the lack of power your hips are not ballistically producing. So it goes without saying you should not try this until your 1H Swing & Catch technique is solid.

| HIP HINGE EXPLOSIVELY | SWING AROUND IN HORSESHOE SHAPE | SWING & CATCH TO OTHER SIDE | REPEAT |

Rotational Hand to Hand (H2H) Swing & Catch: This H2H variation is a perfect example of what's to come in the next chapter now adding a longer arc by pivoting the toes and hips into the mix.

PIVOT FEET & CONTOUR MACE TO ARM   "POP & FLOAT"

CATCH MACEHEAD   FLICK WRIST BACK TO HANDLE

<u>Berserker Snatch & Catch</u>: This is an advanced technique combining my love for both steel maces & kettlebells. In both volumes of my online ebooks: *GADA Swing: Guide For Kettlebell & Steel Mace Strength Training* I teach how to mold these modalities separately and together (calling them Berserker). However, please consider this as an optional bonus exercise. Not only does your kettlebell snatch technique need to be on point, but your hand dexterity will be challenged as one grips the mace head and the other relaxes overhead to let the kettlebell rotate over the wrist (not slamming on the forearm).

Odin is the Norse God of war & poetry (also Thor's father). He gave his eye for knowledge because no sacrifice is too great for wisdom. It is the center piece of Viking Valhalla Training Center for this reason.

That's a 20KG/40LB Steel Mace & 24KG/53LB Kettlebell

CHAPTER 7

VIKING STRIKING

Up to this point in the book, we've gone through a lot of anti-rotational drills and exercises to prime stability and mobility in all the right places. In this chapter, it's all about creating powerful rotation from the ground up. People confuse what real rotation is due to mythical beliefs of twisting your torso back & forth — no reason, no explanation, nothing evidence based. "It works your core" has become a normal saying within the fitness industry all because people crave a flat stomach. A perfect example is the Russian Twist, where a person sits forward flexed on their tail bone with their feet off the ground and then twists their low back with a weight up and over their hips. All I see is the lumbar spine getting torqued and twisted with the coccyx rooted to floor under load. Yet, your trainer says "YEAH! Work that core!" — and you're oblivious to the fact that you're being pushed to an inevitable low back injury all because of the romanticized idea of "it works your core."

Real rotation requires the feet to pivot to fully rotate the hips with power as the upper body produces a simultaneous push & pull effect. This connects the torso with the hips as one piece, and we see this in a lot of classic athletic archetype movements like throwing a ball, kicking, tackling, and various striking positions. Regardless of the position, they all require precision, accuracy, and fluidity in any 3-D plane. So how do we apply this to the steel mace? Since it is naturally offset, it has the characteristics of an axe, hockey stick, and can be used as a tool to help align many positions you would also see in martial arts.

Uppercuts: Set up in the front rack, and raise your mace hand up. Keep your knees soft and elbow strike back still looking forward — pivoting your rear foot in to rotate the hips. Then pull with the base hand and uppercut (push) with your mace hand rotating to the other side. Notice in figures 2 & 4 I have my forearms vertical on either side, and you do not want to let them extend as you rotate left to right. Build your cadence thinking "center, elbow, uppercut, center" and go slow at first. Staying in alignment with the mace is key to building more speed and power as you get better at it. When pivoting your feet think of "squishing a bug" to really dig the toes in. There is no real rotation if the feet aren't pivoting to give the hips power with dynamic push/pull from the upper body.

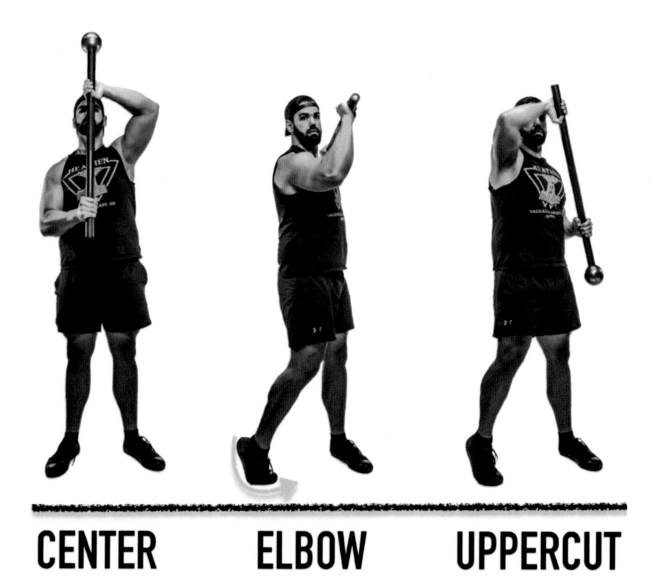

CENTER   ELBOW   UPPERCUT

A common mistake many make with this is looking back and forth in different directions. Notice how my head stays looking forward as if I was going to uppercut someone dead in the chin (this is really easy simply thinking of someone you don't like). Be sure to perform BOTH sides — one side will be more uncoordinated than the other when first practicing these.

PIVOT FEET   **REPEAT**

Ground & Pound: Have both palms down, and have the mace hand with slight elbow flexion and the base hand pulled back near the torso. The feet and hips are pivoted in the start. You will then pull & toss the mace head upward into the vertical stack and simultaneously switch your hands to punch down to the other side. Think you have two punching bags on each side of you and you want to strike them smoothly transitioning left to right.

PULL & TOSS   BRING FEET   SWITCH HANDS IN   PUNCH TOP   "SQUISH THE BUG"
WITH MACE HAND UP   NEUTRAL   VERTICAL STACK   HAND DOWN   PIVOTING FEET

As you punch down with the top mace hand lead with your index and thumb grabbing it in mid air so you don't slam it into the meat of your palm. Then, as you did with the uppercut, remember to actively pull the base hand so your torso can rotate more powerfully with your hips and feet.

78

Once again, the power and fluidity all comes from pivoting your feet left to right. Do not be lazy by passively turning the toes in. Really drive the toes into the ground like you are "squishing a bug" or "putting out a cigarette bud." Keep your eyes on the mace head as it tosses up and punches downward.

Side View of Ground & Pound

Back Step Lunge Uppercuts (L1): Grab the mace both palms down and rotate it around your front leg as your rear leg lunges back digging down with the toes. Once in a strong lunge position, push off your rear leg to push and pull the mace into a tall standing uppercut (like a military stance). Many get caught up thinking only with the mace hand (punching up) and neglect the base hand not pulling it back. By doing so, it keeps your forearms vertical and elbows flexed to keep your body balanced as it chops up and down from the lunge position.

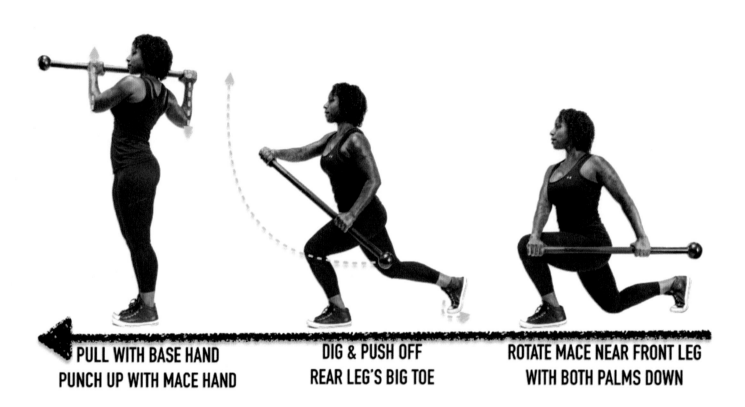

PULL WITH BASE HAND
PUNCH UP WITH MACE HAND

DIG & PUSH OFF
REAR LEG'S BIG TOE

ROTATE MACE NEAR FRONT LEG
WITH BOTH PALMS DOWN

Back & Forth Lunge Uppercuts (L2): This has the same start as the level one version, but progresses with a longer stride with the forward lunge being added in. The key is thinking one foot is stable (with the mace rotating around it) and the other mobile lunging back & forth. Notice in the middle photo how Jemena needs to balance for a split second in order to transition the two front to back lunges smoothly. The same push/pull action is still required at the end range and then reversed back with the same back step lunge stride.

PUSH

PULL

FORWARD LUNGE   UPPERCUT   BACK STEP LUNGE

Hockey Slap Shots (L1 - One Direction): Start in the prayer position and slide the mace hand palm up to strike downward — the base hand will pull in toward the torso. Simultaneously pivot your feet in the slap shot's direction. Keep your head looking forward as you "squish the bug." Really dig the toes down and squeeze the glutes to fully rotate the hips. Do NOT be lazy with your pivoting technique passively twisting the foot. Fully extend your arm punching downward (as if you were going to hit a puck). Smoothly rotate the body back in to the prayer position and repeat. Perform one side at a time and then perform the other to get the groove of this.

| START IN PRAYER POSITION | MACE HAND PALM UP BASE HAND PALM DOWN | "SQUISH THE BUG" PIVOT FEET | PUSH MACE HAND PULL BASE HAND |

Hockey Jump Slap Shots (L2 - Both Directions): Start in the prayer position and jump sliding your hands palm up for the mace hand and palm down simultaneously. As your front foot plants down first, the rear foot will then cross step back as you slap down athletically. Once in the full end range, jump back into the prayer position and look in the other direction performing the same action. This requires quick feet and hands to perform this smoothly. Go slow to build up your rhythm and then add speed.

PRAYER POSITION

PULL WITH BASE HAND

PUSH WITH MACE HAND

CROSS STEP SMOOTHLY LEFT TO RIGHT

Axe Chop Switches: Start with the mace hand palm up with your arm extended out rotationally and base hand palm down with it pulled in near the sternum. To switch to the other side, flip your mace palm down, and as you pivot your feet in the other direction release your base hand to let the bottom handle flip up.

START   **FLIP MACE HAND**   **RELEASE BASE HAND**
                PALM DOWN   **TO LET HANDLE FLIP UP**

The hands with then quickly switch looking toward the other direction as the mace hand punches upward and the base hand, once again, pulls in. You'll repeat it left to right as smoothly as possible.

The key is to think you're performing this in front of a wall. You don't want the mace handle to turn away from your body or else the axis of rotation will be thrown off.

TURN BODY &
PIVOT FEET

SWITCH HAND
POSITION

PUNCH UP WITH MACE HAND
PULL WITH BASE HAND

Before we get into tire striking with a steel mace, it needs to be reiterated that using a sledgehammer is fine because it is a striking tool by nature. Meaning it needs a target to hit each rep to maintain power and accuracy. This works due to its rectangular head shape and short narrow handle to better stay in line with chopping patterns. However with these attributes, it cannot be swung with a continuous centrifugal force like a Gada or steel mace can. View a sledgehammer like a fork and a steel mace like a spoon — you can't have soup using a fork because the head shape doesn't fit the goal. So whether you use a sledgehammer or not the steel mace still serves as a great tire striking modality because of its longer handle (therefore creating a bigger upward arc). It's also casted into one steel piece with zero chance of the head flying off. A couple years ago, I actually witnessed this with a trainer having his client tire striking with a cheap plastic glued sledgehammer. As the client raised it over head at full force, the hammer head detached from the handle and flew off backward nearly hitting the trainer right in the head (it would also have been a guaranteed lawsuit if it had hit anyone else). So with that said, I prefer a steel mace for this reason if you're a fitness coach wanting to integrate tire striking safely with your clients. Most local automotive and tire junk yards in your area are willing to take a small fee or even give tires away for free. You do not need to get a giant 100lb one like I have pictured. Anything more than 50lb with a thick tire diameter will do.

2H Tire Strike: Have your mace hand palm up and base hand palm down. Stand sideways from the tire and arc your mace hand upward overhead. As you pivot the feet and hips, slide your mace hand down (stacking with your base hand). Once the steel mace strikes downward into the tire hinge your hips back to add more power. After it rebounds up, release your mace hand off the handle and stand up catching it (with the same hand) near the mace head. You'll then reset your feet sideways again to repeat the process. You will notice one side will not strike as hard as the other. While this is normal, you'll start to groove it better and better with the same power output with consistent practice overtime.

STAND SIDEWAYS FROM TIRE

ARC MACE UPWARD

SLIDE TOP HAND DOWN & PIVOT REAR FOOT

STRIKE & HIP HINGE

LET TOP HAND RELEASE AFTER STRIKE & CATCH TO REPEAT

Poor Tire Tapping: This is the exact opposite of everything we've been talking about in this chapter, and yet is seen as completely normal to most uneducated trainers because all that matters is "it looks cool." Typically, many face the tire being squared up with it while not rotating their feet and hips. With this lack of power, the top hand doesn't slide and gets muscled downward very un-athletically; causing a rebound shock wave into the arms and shoulders when it taps against the tire. This is why you're supposed to let go of the mace hand the second it strikes sliding down the handle. Then to finish it off . . . it's no surprise this form rounds the low back at the striking point (not hinging from the hip).

What's more disgraceful than the form is the weak tapping sound you hear on the tire. When a tire is struck with power you can automatically tell the difference with an audible strong bounding "*DUNNK!*" or weak "*dink*" sound against the tire's rubber surface. The mace head should also visibly sink into the tire upon being struck (bottom left). In contrast, it's like someone hitting a punching bag with all upper body and flexed wrists (more so slapping it then punching it).

Now is it possible to tire strike rotationally being squared up with it? Yes, but it limits the upward arc with less range and the mace head is at more risk coming back hitting toward the midline of the body. If you notice the most common sport striking and throwing patterns are all sideways from their target to load up more power from the ground up. Not only that, but you can do way more tire striking variations being sideways from it as you'll see on the next pages.

H2H Tire Strike: Start out the same as a 2H tire strike, but after the strike you have to quickly switch your feet and hands as the mace rebounds. Don't try this hand to hand version if your 2H tire strike isn't balanced with even power on both sides. Quick hands and feet must athletically stay in rhythm going left to right smoothly. Go slow so you can find a path before adding speed after catching and resetting the mace each rep.

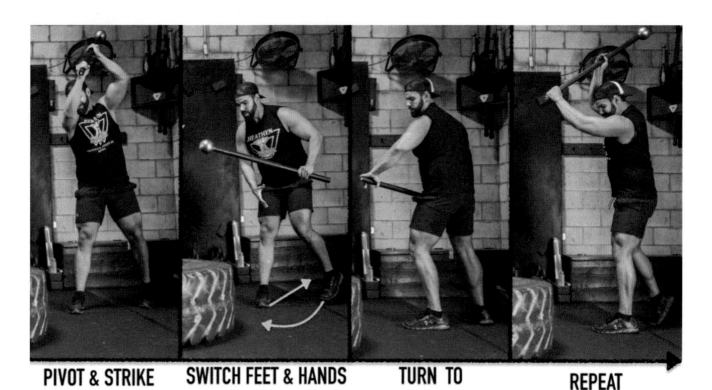

PIVOT & STRIKE   SWITCH FEET & HANDS   TURN TO   REPEAT
                       AS MACE BOUNCES UP   OTHER SIDE

1H Thor Tire Strike: set up just as you would performing a 1H 360, but stand sideways from the tire and push the mace in toward it. From here, we're replacing the pause with a pivot to let your body fully rotate with power. As soon you strike down, hip hinge and catch it with your free hand as the mace rebounds back up. You'll reset it each rep in the 1H vertical stack position. It's highly recommended you use the lightest mace you have to get the technique down first.

SPOT WITH FREE HAND

PUSH

PENDULUM

PULL & PIVOT

STRIKE & HIP HINGE

CATCH & RESET

Tire Wall or Partner Joust: Set up the tire standing vertically near a wall. You want to give a couple inches of space between the tire and wall so it can effectively bounce back and forth with each joust. Once set up, have the mace hand palm up and base hand palm down. Stand sideways with the knees soft and athletic. You will then joust and step out simultaneously striking the top middle of the tire (do not hit the sides or else it will lose the back & forth motion). After each joust, step back the front foot and pull the mace in toward the torso to reload into the lats and repeat. Only use a brick wall or partner (facing opposite from each other) for this tire joust drill.

BASE HAND PALM DOWN
MACE HAND PALM UP

STEP & JOUST
SIMULTANEOUSLY

PULL MACE & FRONT
FOOT BACK TO RELOAD

REPEAT KEEPING TIRE
BOUNCING OFF WALL

PARTNER TIRE JOUST

<u>Partner Tire Joust & Roll</u>: Set up the tire vertically standing up in between you and your partner — facing opposite from each other. Use an open and flat space where it can easily roll 10-15 yards as you both joust it back & forth. Do NOT perform this if your tire can't roll smoothly because of jagged ends or uneven surfaces.

This is a really fun partner drill, but I must warn you it can turn quickly dangerous if your partner is being a jerk. You both need to be on the same page communicating how far the tire is rolling and how hard it is pushed. It is also critical you do NOT lock your knees standing as you joust. If you do, the tire's rolling force will easily crash your knee inward. So stay low bending the knees, focus on stopping the tire, and jousting it back to your partner. Using an interval clock going one minute on jousting and one minute of resting (switching sides for the next set) is best.

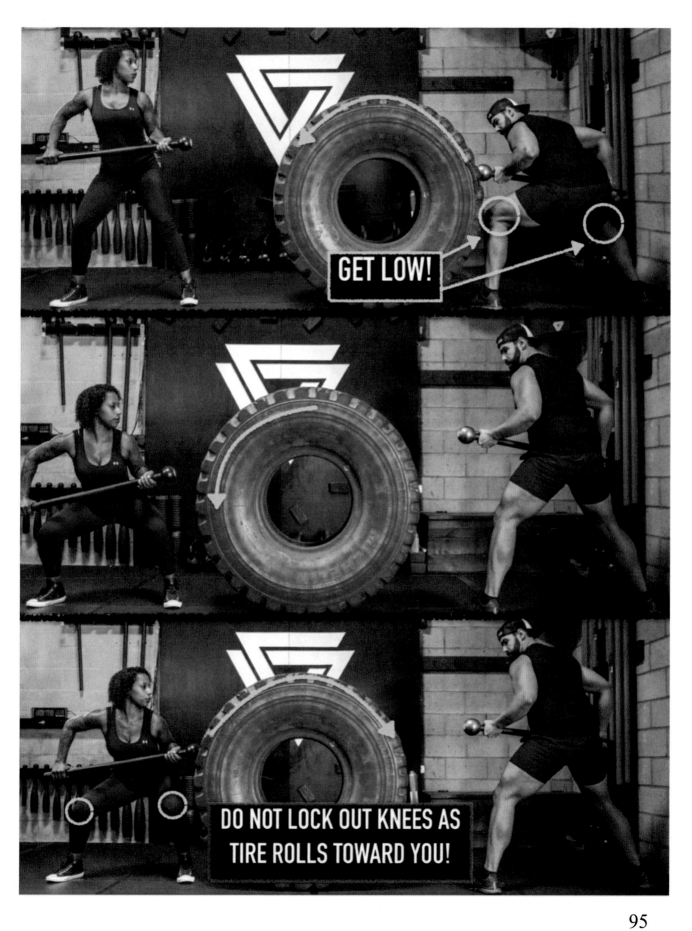

GET LOW!

DO NOT LOCK OUT KNEES AS TIRE ROLLS TOWARD YOU!

CHAPTER 8

INDIAN CLUB
MILL DRILLS

One day in fall of 2010, I was playing a pickup football game at the local park with friends, and it was something I loved doing every Saturday. However, once again, this was during my young & dumb era thinking I was invincible. We played with no pads and you were considered a sissy if you wanted to play "two hand touch" instead of tackling. On the day of this game, I had no idea what pain was coming from stupidly thinking this way. I caught a pass in stride and one person on the opposing team jumped on my right side. As I came down to the ground, my left shoulder slammed and slid into the slick grass . . . with a whole other person's bodyweight still on my hanging right. I vividly remember thinking I was okay as I was getting up, and then could not feel my left arm. It felt like a limp noodle, and I began to freak out after immense shoulder pain set in. After getting home, I spent the next sleepless nights regretting thinking I was invincible to injury and knew that was my last park football game.

After taking a month off from working out with weights to let my left shoulder heal I was dying to get in an "upper body" workout and press heavy that day. I was relieved I could still press 100lb dumbbells overhead, but after my workout I slowly felt the pain come back. The big scary difference this time was now my entire left side was feeling numb all the way down to my left foot. This was honestly more scary than the day of the injury because I thought during this post workout hour I was having a stroke. While I wasn't, I realized that day I was heavily neglecting my joint and nervous systems. It was only after this day I stopped thinking like a meathead and knew I had to figure out a new path for my body to recover from this if I wanted to have a healthy body in the future.

"WHAT DO ALL INJURIES HAVE IN COMMON? YOU DO NOT MOVE THE SAME AFTER"
- DR. PERRY NICKELSTON

During this time, I could not afford health care/physical therapy and was constantly on the bubble of living in my car if I didn't make ends meet (I was working three different jobs and applying to be a firefighter all over Los Angeles County that year). Not only that, I didn't need a doctor to scare me into pain killers and surgery to "recover" in the future. I knew my shoulder was severely injured, but the nerve across it was seriously impinged being crammed into the capsule and clavicle. So I asked myself "what can I do right now?" because I didn't know any realistic solutions yet. Educating myself was only natural at this crucial point to make sure I wasn't going to end up with half my body working. I started reading more anatomy books and looked up online sources for top people in physical therapy. Among those was Dr. Gray Cook and Dr. Ed Thomas and I learned how to assess my body's common movement patterns, find the weak spots, and make them better each day practicing without overkilling my body. What they both had in common was constantly referring Indian clubs. They swung them in directions I'd never seen before and saw patterns my shoulders could get to know better. After getting my first pair of Indian clubs in the mail I was surprised how light they were at 2lb, yet all the mill drills were insanely hard to do for me and I had to start small doing side casts.

Just like the Gada, there is much history to Indian Clubs being utilized in many military and sport programs for warm ups. What makes them extremely unique is they turn your shoulder & elbow into ball joints rather than linear flexion/extension joints you would see in a bicep curl. With my left shoulder becoming stiff and guarded after the injury it was no surprise my elbow and wrist tendons also developed downstream issues becoming weaker. This also made my right side over compensate being more tense. While educating myself, a common transparent saying in handling chronic pain was also apparent: "where you think it is . . . it's not." A good example of this is many thinking stretching is the best method to reduce local low back pain. While it may give relief for a short period its not solving the real issue where you lack strength and stability to help these local points of pain.

If you don't know how to simply brace and neutralize your spine using the right muscles (like in the bird dog and dead bug) it's no surprise you'll have back pain chronically. The same was happening to me for my shoulders taking time off and then repeating the process injuring them again with overload and ego. It becomes a vicious cycle, and you need to break it learning new methods. Indian clubs taught me what I wasn't using to protect shoulders in different articulations with little weight. As Dr. Gray Cook commonly states, "these aren't heavy — they're fast." So learning to groove these speeds with Indian clubs became a ritual for me before every workout. This gave me a new realization of how tools should be utilized in one's programming and why it's becoming a huge myth that steel mace training is ridding shoulder pain with 360s. As we have learned throughout this book — strength is a skill. So just doing 360s is like saying you're gonna jump on a horse and know how to ride it without any instruction (or being an idiot playing tackle football with no pads in my case).

This is why I'm presenting a better and safer option to not only rehab your shoulders, but learn to use a simple tool I think is vastly underrated. With the Indian club's shorter lever we can contain smaller circles around the shoulder, elbow, and wrist in more controlled speeds. What people need to realize is strength should not be deemed on lifting heavy numbers. Professional football quarterbacks and baseball pitchers do not make money on how big their arms are, but more on how fast and accurate they throw the ball. The steel mace requires bigger circles with its long handle and is not something I'd ever recommend to someone with a chronic shoulder injury. Subbing steel mace 360s with these *Indian Club Mill Drills* are highly recommended to those with these issues.

Indian clubs can easily be bought online and are usually made out of wood or polyurethane from 1 to 2lbs. Remember it's about fluidity with Indian clubs — not the weight. Find your path first, then add speed when swinging.

Indian Club Side Cast: Set up in the front rack position with a vertical forearm. Be sure to fully grip the Indian club with a secure grip (not tilting away from the body with a flexed wrist). Your free hand can be placed on your hip so it won't be in the way as the club laterally swings out. Once set, drop the Indian club inward toward the feet and cast out to the side with the arm fully extended. It is very key to have your elbow pit up at the end range so your shoulder doesn't dump inward and stay connected to your lat.

GRIP IN FRONT RACK WITH VERTICAL

KEEP ELBOW PIT UP

SIDE CAST OUT LETTING ELBOW & WRIST EXTEND

Also, notice how my wrist is getting extension and when you swing it back into the front rack it should be neutral with a vertical forearm again. So this is not only beneficial for the shoulders, but the elbow and wrist tendons.

100

Indian Club Inside Mill: Once your side cast feels smooth we can advance it by adding a bigger upward arc that curves back in to the front rack for each rep. Start in the front rack and side cast with more speed so it will arc up higher like holding a torch overhead. Once you reach the optimal height overhead, bend your elbow outward like you're "combing your hair" so the club can pendulum smoothly behind your head. From there, you will need to decelerate it by actively pulling in and circling the elbow into a strong front rack.

2

ARC UP LIKE HOLDING A TORCH

3

"COMB YOUR HAIR"

1

SIDE CAST OUT

4

PULL BACK INTO FRONT RACK

Indian Club Outside Mill: All we're doing here now is performing this mill in reverse from the last variation. You will notice either the inside or outside mill will feel more difficult than the other. To be clear, I refer the elbow dictating which direction it's going.

FRONT RACK   **CIRCLE ELBOW OUT**   **"COMB YOUR HAIR"**

EXTEND ARM OUT LIKE HOLDING A TORCH

SECURE WITH NEUTRAL WRIST

<u>Indian Club Striking Mill:</u> Pullover the club behind your head and forcefully pivot the feet so the arm can extend and strike outward rotationally. From there you need to side cast the club by pivoting the feet in the other direction to smoothly continue the axis of rotation. As you strike the club out each rep you can push & pull your free arm to add more power from the torso.

START IN PULLOVER　　**PIVOT & ROTATE HIPS**　　**STRIKE BY FULLY EXTENDING ARM**

This drill also works exceptionally well for throwing athletes who are rehabbing elbow tendinopathy issues (baseball pitchers, boxers, or football quarterbacks). Notice how my head is looking forward like I have a target to strike or throw to.

SIDE CAST PIVOTING IN OTHER DIRECTION

PULL FREE ARM IN FOR MORE POWER

CHAPTER 9

BEGINNER WORKOUTS

Workouts should always be treated like practice focusing on the critical techniques needed to go the next level. On the following pages are workout blocks on every steel mace exercise we've covered in this book. This steel mace beginner program is set up to test your skills for four weeks with four workouts in each week. This is so your heavy mace will feel like a medium mace by the time you're done with this program. Warm up with the *Prime Nine* drills first, and then perform each exercise in the order they're in. Each one will either require you to perform it in a number of repetitions or seconds for each side. Remember to do both sides with the steel mace, so left and right is equal to one set (not two sets). Sets are relating to work and rest. So for example, when you perform 6-8 offset deadlift reps on your right you'll switch to the left to do another 6-8 reps. Then set the mace down and take a minute or two to rest in between sets. Rounds are where two exercises are performed back and forth. Going without rest is not recommended for these workouts. The reps are low because you're really doing double to perform left and right for each single set.

While there's more advanced movements you can do with a steel mace, rushing beginner skills is the worst thing you can do with a new tool you don't know a lot about yet. Nowadays many hinder their workout plans all because of something cool they saw at the gym or on social media. What you're not seeing are the years of work this person dedicated to these skills you want.

Then as a special bonus, you can download this entire workout program in PDF file format with every exercise hyperlinked to video demos. Every demo is detailed with captions and verbal coaching cues to help you understand each exercise even better. Please download the free QR code app first and then scan it with your mobile device. You will then be sent to a Google Drive link to download the workouts:

Scan to discover !

Download this free Unitag App to scan at unitag.io/app

WORKOUT #1 WEEK 1	REPS / TIME	SETS
DYNAMIC CURLS	PERFORM FOR 30-45 SECONDS	3-4 SETS
OFFSET DEADLIFTS	6-8 REPS EACH SIDE	4-5 SETS L & R = 1 SET
OFFSET MILITARY PRESSES	6-8 REPS EACH SIDE	4- 5 SETS L & R = 1 SET
LAP SQUATS	6-8 REPS EACH SIDE	4- 5 SETS L & R = 1 SET

WORKOUT #2 WEEK 1	REPS / TIME	SETS
UPPERCUTS	6-8 REPS EACH SIDE	3 SETS L & R = 1 SET
PENDULUMS	PERFORM FOR 30-45 SECONDS	3-4 SETS L & R = 1 SET
BENT OVER ROWS	6-8 REPS EACH SIDE	3-4 SETS L & R = 1 SET
GROUND & POUND	PERFORM FOR 30-45 SECONDS	3-4 SETS

WORKOUT #3 WEEK 1	REPS	ROUNDS
SUMO SIDE LUNGES + UPPERCUT BACK STEP LUNGES	5 REPS EACH SIDE + 5 REPS EACH SIDE	4 ROUNDS
2H 360s + 1H SWING & CATCH	10 REPS EACH SIDE + 10 REPS EACH SIDE	4 ROUNDS

WORKOUT #4 WEEK 1	REPS	SETS
2H TIRE STRIKE	5 REPS EACH SIDE	3-4 SETS L & R = 1 SET
HOCKEY SLAP SHOT L1	10 REPS EACH SIDE	3-4 SETS L & R = 1 SET
AXE CHOP SWITCHES	10 REPS EACH SIDE	3-4 SETS L & R = 1 SET
2H TIRE STRIKE (AGAIN)	5 REPS EACH SIDE	3-4 SETS L & R = 1 SET

WORKOUT #5 WEEK 2	REPS / TIME	SETS
SUMO SIDE STEP LUNGES	PERFORM FOR 30-45 SECONDS	3-4 SETS
OFFSET DEADLIFT TO BENT OVER ROW	6-8 REPS EACH SIDE	4-5 SETS L & R = 1 SET
PENDULUM TO OFFSET MILITARY PRESS	6-8 REPS EACH SIDE	4-5 SETS L & R = 1 SET
FRONT SQUATS	6-8 REPS EACH SIDE	4-5 SETS L & R = 1 SET

WORKOUT #6 WEEK 2	REPS	SETS – ROUNDS
UPPERCUTS	6-8 REPS EACH SIDE	3-4 SETS L & R = 1 SET
2H HALF KNEELING 360s	6-8 REPS EACH SIDE	3-4 SETS L & R = 1 SET
90/90 HIP PRESS 360s	6-8 REPS EACH SIDE	3-4 SETS L & R = 1 SET

WORKOUT #7 WEEK 2	REPS / TIME	ROUNDS
2H 360 TO SIDE STEP LUNGE + UPPERCUT BACK STEP LUNGES	5 REPS EACH SIDE + 5 REPS EACH SIDE	4-5 ROUNDS
1H 360s + H2H SWING & CATCH	6-8 REPS EACH SIDE + PERFORM FOR 30-45 SEC	4-5 ROUNDS

WORKOUT #8 WEEK 2	REPS / TIME	SETS – ROUNDS
TIRE JOUSTS	10 REPS EACH SIDE	3 SETS
HOCKEY SHUFFLE SHOT L2	PERFORM FOR 30-45 SECONDS	3 SETS L & R = 1 SET
AXE CHOP SWITCHES	PERFORM FOR 30-45 SECONDS	3 SETS L & R = 1 SET
H2H TIRE STRIKE	PERFORM FOR 30-45 SECONDS	3 SETS

WORKOUT #9 WEEK 3	REPS	SETS
2H 360 TO DYNAMIC CURL	10 REPS EACH SIDE	3 SETS L & R = 1 SET
OFFSET DEADLIFT TO BENT OVER ROW	6-8 REPS EACH SIDE	4-5 SETS L & R = 1 SET
2H 10 & 2's	6-8 REPS EACH SIDE	3 SETS L & R = 1 SET
PRESSOUT SQUATS	5 REPS EACH SIDE	3 SETS L & R = 1 SET

WORKOUT #10 WEEK 3	REPS / TIME	SETS – ROUNDS
2H 360 TO FRONT BACK STEP LUNGE	5 REPS	5 SETS
1H 360s	5 REPS EACH SIDE	5 SETS L & R = 1 SET
H2H 10 & 2's	PERFORM FOR 30-45	5 SETS

WORKOUT #11 WEEK 3	REPS / TIME	ROUNDS
BACK & FORTH UPPERCUT LUNGES + GROUND & POUND	5 REPS EACH SIDE + PERFORM FOR 30-45 SECONDS	4 ROUNDS
SIDE LUNGE H2H 10 & 2's + H2H ROTATIONAL SWING & CATCH	PERFORM FOR 30 SEC + PERFORM FOR 30 SEC	4 ROUNDS

WORKOUT #12 WEEK 3	REPS / TIME	SETS – ROUNDS
H2H TIRE STRIKES	PERFORM FOR 30-45 SECONDS	3-4 SETS
HOCKEY SHUFFLE SHOT L2 + AXE CHOP SWITCHES	PERFORM FOR 30 SEC + PERFORM FOR 30 SEC	4-5 ROUNDS
THOR TIRE STRIKES	3-5 REPS EACH SIDE	3 SETS L & R = 1 SET

WORKOUT #13 WEEK 4	REPS / TIME	SETS
90/90 HIP PRESS 360s	6-8 REPS EACH SIDE	4-5 SETS L & R = 1 SET
GROUND & POUND	PERFORM FOR 30-45 SECONDS	4-5 SETS
GOBLET SQUATS	6-8 REPS EACH SIDE	4-5 SETS

WORKOUT #14 WEEK 4	REPS	SETS
BACK & FORTH LUNGE UPPERCUTS	5 REPS EACH SIDE	5 SETS L & R = 1 SET
360 KNEELING COMPLEX	5 REPS EACH SIDE	5 SETS L & R = 1 SET
BACK & FORTH LUNGE UPPERCUTS (AGAIN)	5 REPS EACH SIDE	5 SETS L & R = 1 SET

WORKOUT #15 WEEK 4	REPS	SETS - ROUNDS
H2H 360 TO BACK STEP LUNGE + UPPERCUTS	5 REPS EACH SIDE + 10 REPS EACH SIDE	4 ROUNDS
BERSERKER SNATCH & CATCH (OPTIONAL)	6-8 REPS EACH SIDE	5 SETS L & R = 1 SET

WORKOUT #16 WEEK 4	REPS / TIME	SETS - ROUNDS
H2H TIRE STRIKES + H2H 10 & 2's	PERFORM FOR 30 SEC + PERFORM FOR 30 SEC	4-5 ROUNDS
TIRE JOUSTS	10 REPS EACH SIDE	4-5 SETS L & R = 1 SET
THOR TIRE STRIKES	3-5 REPS EACH SIDE	4-5 SETS L & R = 1 SET

CHAPTER 10

FAQ & ONLINE CONTENT

"So what brands of Steel Maces do you recommend?"

Due to the nature of people pushing copyright infringements now more than ever I do not want to mention any company names in this book (not in the mood to re-print if it happens). However, I have a YouTube video titled: *Steel Mace Training FAQ with Coach Vaughn* mentioning brands I use and recommend to give you more details. Steel Maces are not commonly sold in stores, but can easily be bought online by typing it into any search engine.

When picking a brand, read reviews and make sure that they have capped bottom ends and have a solid 2 inch handle diameter (commonly 36 to 40 inches tall). These are red flags I've seen from poorly done production from the company to save more money. An empty bottom handle makes the steel mace rust from the inside faster and makes it sound like a baby rattle from debris getting inside it. Then small diameter handles will effect your grip positions and will warp overtime.

"So why no sledgehammers again?"

I don't mind you using one for tire striking because it's a striking tool. I used sledgehammers a lot in Fire & Rescue Academies for forceable entry techniques. However, the issue is it being confused for the same methods as Traditional Gada or Steel Mace Training.

To this day, I still get "just use a sledgehammer stupid" comments on my social media channels as steel maces get more popular. This is a comment you need to be ready take when investing into steel mace training and educate nay sayers on the very clear differences between the two. Ask, "are smart phones the same as landline phones?" No, completely different features and it's easy to judge a book by it's cover with no education. Steel maces are NOT more expensive either, and I laugh when a person is saying this holding a $1,000 smart phone like they're on a real budget.

"Can I pair the Steel Mace with my Kettlebell Workouts?"

Yes, I personally fell in love with steel maces because they flip the script with the kettlebell swing. Your shoulders are stable and the hips are mobile when ballistically swinging a kettlebell, but with a steel mace 360 your hips are now stable and the shoulders are mobile. I loved this concept so much I made my first ebook based on it: *GADA Swing: Guide For Kettlebell & Steel Mace Strength Training*, and then a second volume evolving into kettlebell doubles & Heavy Mace Training. So if you're looking for more guidance on programming the two together I would highly advise getting the ebook once finished with this program.

"What about Barbarian Squats and Grave Diggers?"

These, in my opinion, are the most overrated and poorly performed movements you can do with a steel mace. A "Barbarian Squat" is where you push it overhead from the vertical stack and then forcefully pull it back into a squat position. The problem is it encourages you to duck your head and round the mid back in order to get the mace's long handle behind your body. This is where a steel club would suffice better with a pullover over to one side and then pressed out into a squat with its short handle.

Grave Diggers make no sense to replicate digging with a shovel. Pretend to dip the mace head toward the ground rounding your back and then raise it up over head back & forth. Unless you plan on digging your own grave literally . . . it's not an ideal skill many want to develop. While I understand the idea of an upward chopping pattern — at the end of the day a mace is still not a shovel, and I would rather save this effort on my garden. Tire striking with a steel mace develops real chopping power and is why many suck at chopping wood. I do NOT recommend these exercises at all.

"Steel mace doubles (two at the same time)?"

With the popularity of steel maces growing more and more each year it's no surprise many will overcomplicate them with double steel mace 360s. Now is there a problem with this? Not really, but ask yourself what can you can do with steel mace doubles beyond that? The inventory of movements you can do with double maces is VERY short. Please don't be the "well actually!" guy coming up with a bunch of random double mace circus tricks. If you really want to get into doubles from a steel mace influence . . . try steel clubs. The club's shorter handles allow you to swing them in multiple positions the mace can't. The barbell bar is also a great tool, but you don't see experienced lifters using two of those at the same time either.

STEEL CLUB SEESAW MILLS

For more content with the steel mace being infused with other fitness tools I have four separate ebooks that have 130+ exercises featured in each one with in-depth video tutorials all hyperlinked in PDF file format to be downloaded on either smartphone or desktop. You can see more of their features @ CoachVaughn.net

Be sure to check out my second paperback book, *The Kettlebell Awaits*, also available on Amazon.

A big special thanks to Jemena, Amanda, and my photographer Anabel, for these incredible high definition photos she captured. If you're serious about getting in a photoshoot for your business — I would HIGHLY recommend her — Website @ Deliquesceflux.com

Please feel free to use any of these hashtags on social media to help spread the word of *Enter The Steel Mace*. Thank you for purchasing this book and please leave an Amazon Review of what you think:

#COACHVAUGHN

#ENTERTHESTEELMACE

Made in the USA
Las Vegas, NV
16 December 2023

82921907R00071